YOU CHOOSE

CAN YOU SURVIVE
the 1925 Tri-State
TORNADO?

AN INTERACTIVE HISTORY ADVENTURE

by Matthew K. Manning

CAPSTONE PRESS
a capstone imprint

Published by Capstone Press, an imprint of Capstone.
1710 Roe Crest Drive
North Mankato, Minnesota 56003
capstonepub.com

Library of Congress Cataloging-in-Publication Data is
available on the Library of Congress web site.
ISBN 9781666390797 (library binding)
ISBN 9781666390780 (paperback)
ISBN 9781666390940 (ebook PDF)

Summary: On March 18, 1925, the deadliest tornado in history tore a path through
Missouri, Illinois, and Indiana. The giant twister destroyed several towns and
killed hundreds of people. Will you run to your basement or try to outrun the
tornado in your new Model T car? Do you take your family to the nearby storm
shelter or try to get to your sturdy church before it's too late? With dozens of
possible choices, YOU will have to decide how you'll survive the deadliest tornado
ever recorded in the United States.

Editorial Credits
Editor: Aaron Sautter; Designer: Bobbie Nuytten; Media Researcher: Donna
Metcalf; Production Specialist: Whitney Schaefer

All internet sites appearing in back matter were available and accurate when this
book was sent to press.

TABLE OF CONTENTS

ABOUT YOUR ADVENTURE

YOU are in the path of the deadliest tornado to ever touch down in the United States. The giant twister struck Tornado Alley on March 18, 1925. Whether you are living in Missouri, Illinois, or Indiana, there's no avoiding the Tri-State Tornado. Will you and your family survive this monster storm? Or will you fall victim to its deadly winds as it races across three states?

Chapter One sets the scene. Then you choose which path to read. Follow the directions at the bottom of the page as you read the stories. The decisions you make determine what happens next. After you finish one path, go back and read the others for new perspectives and more adventures.

Turn the page to begin your adventure.

Tornadoes are common during summer months. About 1,000 tornadoes are reported in the United States each year.

CHAPTER 1
THE TURNING WINDS

There are no warnings. You have no time to prepare. It is March 18, 1925, and the deadliest tornado in history is heading your way.

Tornadoes are something of a mystery in 1925. Today, we know the storms form when cold, dry air moving in one direction meets wet, warmer air going in the opposite direction. The warm air rises rapidly as the cool air sinks, causing the winds to spin.

As they reach the ground, these funnel-shaped storms officially become tornadoes. With winds that can spin up to 300 miles (483 kilometers) per hour, they are terrifying forces of nature.

Turn the page.

Even in the 1920s, people know that most tornadoes fade away soon after they contact the ground. So when a tornado touches down briefly in Ellington, Missouri, and returns to the sky, most people think the worst is over. But the truth is, the storm is just getting started.

The storm quickly touches down again and stays on the ground for an unprecedented three and a half hours. It will travel more than 200 miles (320 km) across Missouri, Illinois, and Indiana.

The monster twister will kill hundreds of people and injure thousands of others along the way. Eventually, it will become known as the Tri-State Tornado.

The morning of March 18 begins as any day in the Midwest. Farmers tend to their fields. School teachers go through lessons with their students in class. Store owners open up their shops to serve customers.

Elsewhere, coal miners descend into dark tunnels. Even a bank robbery is being planned. None of these people realize that everything they know is about to change.

As the tornado rages through your town, you must use your wits and quick thinking to stay alive. Every choice you make will determine if you survive, or if you are another casualty of the deadliest tornado in history.

To face the tornado as a coal miner, turn to page 11.

To seek shelter as an elementary student, turn to page 43.

To brave the twister with your brother, turn to page 69.

Underground mining was a difficult and dirty job in the 1920s. Miners usually had to eat their lunches in the depths of the mine.

CHAPTER 2
THE MINES OF MISSOURI

You sit down on the bench and open your lunch pail. You're hot and dirty, and your stomach hurts. You sigh. You're definitely coming down with the same sickness your daughter has. You knew you shouldn't have come to work at the mine today.

Even so, you figure you should try to eat something. As you take a bite of your sandwich, you notice a small piece of paper under your apple. You take it out and unfold the little note. It's a stick figure drawing of a man.

The drawing is labeled with a few messy words. "Daddy by Ellie" it says. One of the *D*'s is backward. Even though she's sick, your little girl packed you a pick-me-up note.

Turn the page.

You smile. If she can manage that, you can probably manage another day in the mine.

A raindrop hits your forehead. You look up, and another lands squarely between your eyes.

"Told you," says the man sitting next to you. You've known Buddy Samuels for most of your life. You both grew up in the small town of Annapolis, Missouri. These days, you and Buddy both work here at the lead mine in the outpost of Leadanna.

"Told me what?" you ask.

"Told you that we were due for a storm," says Buddy through a mouthful of bread.

"You should take that show on the road," you say. "Come see Buddy Samuels and his amazing weather predictions!" you shout in your best carnival barker voice. Buddy, however, is not amused.

"Hey, I haven't been wrong yet," says Buddy.

He takes another bite of his sandwich. You put yours down as a sudden wave of nausea hits you.

"You look a little pale, there," Buddy says.

"Yeah," you say. "I think I've got whatever the stomach bug is going around."

"If I were you, I'd head home," says Buddy. "A bad rain's coming."

"I'm good," you say. "I think."

"Well, better make up your mind. It's almost 12:30. Time to get back to it," Buddy nods toward the mine entrance. "That stuff's not gonna dig itself outta the ground."

To keep working at the mine, turn to page 14.

To go home instead, turn to page 19.

You take a swig of water from your metal cup. Then you stand up and stretch. *I'll be fine*, you think to yourself. You can't really afford to miss work anyway. Your wife and daughter depend on the 80 cents an hour you bring home. You trudge back toward the mine.

Soon, you're lowered down into the mine on a primitive elevator. It's not often you think about electricity, but today you're glad the mine has it. Feeling as sick as you do, the thought of walking down a long, unstable staircase sounds awful.

At the bottom, you head down a dark tunnel. You carry a small electric lamp to light the way. You trudge by dozens of wooden supports that look like large door frames. Soon you enter a huge chamber. The clanging sounds of pickaxes hitting rock and a screaming drill echo around you.

There are columns of rocks here and there. They're meant to keep the ceiling from collapsing. But they make the large chamber look like some ancient Greek temple. Although crude, the pillars make this space feel manmade.

Turn the page.

Miners used several tools, such as hammers, drills, pickaxes, and shovels, to break up rock and dig out the ore.

You walk by the men using the drill, then wait until another man pushes a metal cart full of lead ore down a track. You carefully step over the track and place your lamp on the ground.

Then you pick up your pickaxe and begin chipping away at the lead deposits hiding in the chamber's wall. After a few minutes, you're feeling even weaker than before. You must truly be sick.

Then you hear a call from across the chamber. "Hey! The lift is out!" You're a bit grateful for the interruption. You put your pickaxe down and follow the other miners back to the elevator.

On your way, you see the electric lights strung up on the ceiling aren't working. Something has happened above ground.

Despite feeling like you might not make it, you turn and head toward a different tunnel. You start to climb a tall wooden staircase to the surface.

However, you're not prepared for what you see once you reach the top. Or rather, you're not prepared for what you *don't* see.

The main building is just a pile of rubble. There had to be a dozen people inside when it collapsed. But now all you can see are piles of broken wood and plaster.

"It was a tornado!" a terrified man says from behind you.

"A tornado," you say softly, almost under your breath.

"That's right, and it's headed straight for town!" the man exclaims.

You focus on the rubble of the main building. You should help those trapped under the debris. Survivors could be injured. They could be running out of air.

Turn the page.

Then you think of the little drawing in your lunch pail. Your wife and daughter are at home in your small house in Annapolis. That means the storm is heading right for them. Or worse, it could have already hit the town. You need to find out if your family is okay. But you can't just abandon your coworkers either.

To go check on your family, turn to page 21.

To look for survivors in the rubble, turn to page 27.

There's a knot in your gut that just won't go away. You can't spend your day shoveling lead ore or pushing heavy carts up and down the mine's tunnel. No, you're better off going home and getting some sleep.

It's easy to convince your boss to let you off for the day. Your skin is pale and there's a steady sweat on your forehead. You tell him you'll do your best to get to work tomorrow. Then you walk toward your Model T.

You love your car. It's the first one you've ever had. Work has been steady since the mine opened. So you splurged a little and bought this vehicle. The only problem is that you have to constantly wipe the seats clean after the workday is done.

You feel the wind on your face as you drive. Some of the light rain is sprinkling in, but it feels good. You somehow feel hot and cold at the same time. You really must be sick with something.

Turn the page.

The drive is fairly short to Second Street. Soon enough you see your small two-story house. You pull into the lane, which is really just two dirt paths carved into the grass by your car's tires. You stretch and then head inside.

As you do, you notice the sky. It seems darker than usual. You look down the road and see a strange black mass of clouds. This doesn't look like a simple storm to you. It might be worth taking some precautions, but you don't want to alarm anyone.

To take the storm seriously, turn to page 23.

To dismiss the clouds as a harmless storm, turn to page 25.

Your Model T is parked in the lot by the mine's entrance. Luckily, your car wasn't carried away by the tornado. You start it up and speed toward downtown Annapolis. You need to make sure your family is safe.

As you turn into town, you can't believe your eyes. There is no town there! Where a small strip of homes, shops, and restaurants once stood, only hints of the buildings remain. It's as if they were just washed away by an ocean's tide.

You drive slower, despite your desire to get home. You're simply in shock. There were probably eighty to ninety houses in your town. Now, you can count the remaining buildings on your fingers.

You pull up to the lot where your own house should be standing. Broken boards lay in jumbled piles. A fallen tree rests where your living room used to be. There's no sign of your wife or your daughter, Ellie.

Turn the page.

The powerful tornado destroyed many neighborhoods and left little standing.

You slowly push open the door of your Model T and get out. You can't believe your eyes. Then you hear your wife's voice.

"You're okay!" she shouts. She and your daughter run out of the neighbor's yard. They must have been hiding in Mrs. Flint's cellar. You sprint over and hug them both. Your house is gone, but your family—your true home—remains.

THE END

To follow another path, turn to page 9.
To learn more about the Tri-State Tornado, turn to page 101.

"That's no rain cloud," you say under your breath. Instead of walking, you jog through your house's back door. "A storm's coming!" you say to your wife, Melinda. She's sitting in the living room reading a novel. She looks surprised to see you. This is your daughter's naptime. Your wife was planning on enjoying some time to herself.

"What are you doing home?" Melinda asks.

"I think I'm sick, but that's not the problem right now," you say. You go to the window and open the curtains. It's darker outside now than it was just minutes ago. The rain is coming down in sheets. "Doesn't the weather look strange to you? I think we should get somewhere safe."

Melinda walks over to you. She feels your forehead with the back of her hand. "You're burning up!" she says. "You shouldn't be going anywhere."

Turn the page.

"Don't the Flints have a cellar?" you ask.

"Yes," says Melinda.

"Maybe we should ask them if we could hunker down in there. Just until this passes."

"And what if you get the neighbors sick?" asks your wife.

"Well, okay," you say. "How about we get Ellie and go for a drive. Maybe we can outrun this thing if it's what I think it is."

"And what's that?" asks Melinda.

"A tornado," you say.

To go to the neighbor's cellar, turn to page 35.
To try and outrun the storm, turn to page 38.

The rain is coming down pretty hard. But to you, it's just another spring shower. It doesn't seem like something to worry about.

"You're home early," your wife, Melinda, says when you walk into your living room.

"I think I'm coming down with something," you say. "Do we have any more of that bismuth syrup?"

"Oh," Melinda thinks for a moment. "I gave the last of it to Ellie this morning."

"No problem," you say. "I'll run to the store."

"Now?" asks Melinda. "It's pouring out."

"I'll be quick," you say.

The corner store is only a block from your house. You decide to jog there quickly through the rain. Your stomach isn't a big fan of this choice. But you do your best to ignore its rumblings.

Turn the page.

The bell above the door rings as you enter the store. "What are you doing?" asks the store owner, Mr. Anderson.

"Just stopping in for a—"

"Didn't you see the sky?" Mr. Anderson cuts you off. "Come on, get down in my storeroom!"

You look out the front window. The sky is dark, but it just looks like a thick fog. You don't understand what the panic is all about.

To ignore Mr. Anderson, turn to page 29.

To follow him into the storeroom, turn to page 31.

Your stomach churns. And you feel weak from walking up the mine's staircase. But compared to the people trapped in the collapsed building, you're in the best of health. You get to work alongside your fellow miners, lifting heavy boards and bricks to search for survivors.

"Hello!" you call. When you don't hear an answer, you get back to lifting. Then finally, you here something.

"Here!" You hear a voice shout from the rubble. You climb over some boards and push a large metal air duct out of the way.

"Here!" the voice shouts again. The sound is coming from right below your feet.

You pull at the board under you. It strains your back, but you keep lifting. Finally, the board budges. Underneath lies a man. His head is bleeding. It looks bad.

Turn the page.

"Help! We need help here!" you shout.

A woman rushes over. You recognize her. She's the nurse who helped Buddy when he hit his leg with his pickaxe by accident. You and the nurse pull the man from the rubble. Then she gets to work bandaging his head.

A few people in Leadanna and Annapolis died that day. But thanks to your efforts, this injured man wasn't one of them. Soon enough, you head home and find your wife and daughter. They're alive, but your house is in ruins. In the end, that seems like a small price to pay.

THE END

To follow another path, turn to page 9.
To learn more about the Tri-State Tornado,
turn to page 101.

There's a sharp pain in your stomach. Whatever is bothering Mr. Anderson, you want nothing to do with it. All you can think about is getting some medicine and going to sleep. But when Mr. Anderson retreats to his storeroom, buying anything is out of the question. There's no one to ring you up at the cash register.

With a cloudy head and an uneasy stomach, you turn to leave. You push the door open. Outside, the whole downtown appears to be caught in a thick fog. Then you hear the sound of thunder behind you.

You spin around and see a large tornado tearing through the street. It's less than a block away from where you're standing!

You try to run, but you don't get far. You feel yourself lift off the ground. Then you're flung like a ragdoll through the air.

Turn the page.

The powerful tornado hit Annapolis, Missouri, at about 1:15 p.m.

You don't feel yourself land. In fact, you never feel anything again. You've become one of the first victims of the Tri-State Tornado. You only hope that your wife and daughter don't suffer the same fate.

THE END

To follow another path, turn to page 9.
To learn more about the Tri-State Tornado, turn to page 101.

"What are you waiting for?" yells Mr. Anderson. "There's a tornado coming!"

There's something in Mr. Anderson's impatient voice. You take him seriously. You follow him to the back of the store. Then you freeze in your tracks. If there's a tornado on its way, your wife and daughter are back home with no protection.

"I'll be right back!" you shout. With an energy you didn't know you still had, you race out of the small shop.

You don't get halfway down the block before you see your wife. She has your daughter in her arms and is rushing toward you.

"What are you doing?" you shout to her through the rain.

"Trying to find you!" she shouts back. "We need to get home and out of this!" she yells.

Turn the page.

"No!" You take her hand. You run back to the store. Melinda follows you without argument.

When you swing the front door open, you can't even hear the bell over the roaring wind. You and Melinda rush to the back of the store. You open a door and head down a tiny staircase into a dark basement.

"What took you so long?" says Mr. Anderson. He takes Melinda's hand and helps her down the stairs.

It's dark in the storeroom, but it's dry. You take your sleepy daughter from Melinda so she can sit down in the corner. Then you sit by her with your daughter on your lap and the storage shelves to your back.

"It's a tornado," you say.

"It doesn't look like any I've ever seen," Melinda says. "But I believe it."

The howling wind upstairs grows louder—
then louder still.

"I hope Marsha and the girls are okay back
home," Mr. Anderson says.

Before you can reply, you hear creaking
boards above you. Then there's a sound like a
herd of stampeding cattle as the ceiling caves in.

After a short time, the wind dies down, and
your eyes adjust to the darkness. You can see
Melinda, Ellie, and even Mr. Anderson are all
alive and well.

The ceiling collapsed, but the large shelves
behind you are holding up many of the boards
over your head. There's a crack between the
boards behind you. You stand up as best you can
and shove the boards aside. Sunlight shines in.
A few minutes later, you're the last one to crawl
out of the rubble that was once the shop.

Turn the page.

The storm passed through town in less than a minute. Now, it is somehow bright and sunny. But every building you can see is in the same state as Mr. Anderson's store. Annapolis, Missouri, is gone. Only its people remain. But at this moment, that's more than enough.

THE END

To follow another path, turn to page 9.
To learn more about the Tri-State Tornado,
turn to page 101.

You go to your neighbor's house and knock on the door.

"Oh, hello," says Mrs. Flint, as she opens the door. "Is there something I can . . ."

Her voice trails off when she sees how dark it is outside. It's barely after 1:00 p.m. The sky shouldn't look like that.

"I think there's a tornado coming," you say.

"I think you might be right," says Mrs. Flint. "Around back. All of you."

You do as Mrs. Flint says. You've seen the cellar doors behind her home many times. You often wished your own house had such a basement.

You and Melinda quickly round the house. In her arms, Melinda cradles a very sleepy Ellie. The rain is coming down harder now.

Turn the page.

Mrs. Flint reappears at her back door carrying a lantern. She runs to the cellar doors and throws them open. You and Melinda follow her down into the dark, windowless basement and slam the doors shut behind you. The wind makes that a harder task than you thought it would be.

Underground cellars were one of the few places that could provide shelter during a strong storm in the Midwest.

As Mrs. Flint lights the lantern, you huddle against the wall with your wife. Then everything happens in a blur. The wind roars outside. The cellar doors rattle so hard it seems they'll be torn off. You lean over your family to keep them safe.

Finally, the noise quiets down outside. You slowly open the cellar doors to peek outside. You see that the tornado has ripped away Mrs. Flint's entire home!

You leave the cellar and walk across the rubble with your family. Across the street, there's hardly a trace of where your house once stood. At that moment, you feel the queasiness in your stomach return. But it doesn't bother you. It's just a reminder that you're still very much alive.

THE END

To follow another path, turn to page 9.
To learn more about the Tri-State Tornado, turn to page 101.

You decide not to bother the Flint family. Maybe you're making a bigger deal of this than it really is. It's not worth getting another family sick.

However, you'd rather be safe than sorry. So you tell Melinda to take Ellie and pile in your Model T. You back out onto the street and drive away in the opposite direction of the storm clouds. The rain keeps pounding against your windshield.

"Are you sure we should be out in this?" asks Melinda.

It's hard to hear her over the noise of the storm. So you just nod in response.

The wind blows against the side of your car. You adjust your steering to avoid swerving off the road. But it's rough going. You press your foot down harder on the gas pedal. You need to get away from this storm as fast as you can.

You speed down a country road outside of town. But the wind and rain follow. You look at the dashboard and see that you're driving 40 miles per hour. That's as fast as you've ever gotten your car to go.

"Oh my—" you hear your wife say. She's staring out the back window.

You take a quick glance over your shoulder. A giant funnel of a tornado is plowing through the road. It's hard to see through the clouds and mist. But even with just a quick look, there's no mistaking it.

You press the gas pedal as far as it will go. The car bumps and bounces over the rough road. You don't dare look back again. If you do, you could crash the car. But then the wind hits your car, and you feel it sway sideways.

Turn the page.

Suddenly, you feel yourself lurch forward. The car door falls open as your Model T rises into the air. You're spinning so fast, you can't tell which direction is up.

Then just as suddenly, the car slams back into the ground. It lands on its side as if tossed there by a giant having a tantrum. Your head hits the dashboard, and your whole world goes dark.

Luckily, your wife and daughter were thrown from the Model T as it spun in the air. They both landed near the side of the road. Your wife's leg is broken, but your daughter barely has a scratch on her. But unfortunately for you, you'll never open your eyes again.

The tornado was traveling nearly 70 miles per hour. You never had a chance to outrun it in your Model T. Only four people died in the area during the storm. Unfortunately, you were one of them.

THE END

To follow another path, turn to page 9.
To learn more about the Tri-State Tornado,
turn to page 101.

In the 1920s, children in the Midwest often attended small country schoolhouses.

CHAPTER 3
A SCHOOLHOUSE IN DANGER

Your eyelids are heavy. You lean forward, resting your cheek on the palm of your hand. A light rain patters outside. You try to concentrate as Miss Bengert goes over the math lesson again. You keep coming back to the same thought. Why did you stay up so late last night reading that book, *The Boxcar Children*?

As you struggle to keep your eyes open, you regret that decision more than ever. It's early afternoon on March 18, 1925. You're just one of twenty-five kids at your school, Garver Elementary. You just finished lunch, and you're cozy in the small, warm schoolroom. Your eyes begin to close . . .

Turn the page.

"I'm sorry, am I boring you?" Miss Bengert says.

"Um . . . oh . . . no, ma'am," you manage to say.

"Maybe you'd like to come to the blackboard and show the class how this problem is done," says Miss Bengert.

You stand up and walk to the chalkboard. You do your best to stifle a yawn.

The blackboard in front of you is covered with chalk marks. You try to figure out what it all means, like an adventurer trying to understand an ancient scroll. The problem is long division. You hate long division.

"Oh . . . oh my," says Miss Bengert. At first, you think she's talking about you. But when you turn around, you see that she's looking out the window. "What is that?" she asks no one in particular.

"Those are just storm clouds," says Janet from her seat.

The sky outside is strangely dark. It looks as if a sort of gray fog is moving toward the school.

"Children, everyone get under your desks right away," says Miss Bengert. There's something in her voice you've never heard before—panic.

"It's a tornado!" she says.

Turn the page.

Your dad once told you the safest place to be in a tornado is in a cellar or basement. Your school doesn't have either of those. If that is a tornado heading this way, you don't think you'll be safe where you are.

You look at the door to the small school. Then you look at your teacher. She's helping everyone get under their desks. You're not sure that's the best idea. Maybe you should take your chances outside.

To do as the teacher says, go to page 47.

To ignore her and run outside, turn to page 50.

You decide Miss Bengert knows best. You run back and duck under your desk. It's a heavy wooden thing, bolted down to the floor. You do your best to get as far under it as possible.

Outside, you hear the wind pick up. The noise gets louder and louder. It sounds like a train heading right for you.

"Everyone stay calm!" shouts Miss Bengert over the noise. You can barely hear her.

Out of curiosity, you pop your head out from under your desk and take a look. Outside the window, it looks like it's nighttime.

"Under your desk!" the teacher shouts at you. You follow her orders.

You can't hear anything but the roaring wind. Then the school's windows shatter. You hear a crunching sound, followed by a screeching of wood and brick. The whole room seems to shake.

Turn the page.

You cover your head with your hands and curl up into a ball. You squeeze your eyes shut tight. The floor feels like it's moving. You feel the rushing wind and stinging dirt hitting you. You try to open your eyes to take a look, but all you see is gray dust and dirt. Something gets in your eyes, and you shut them tight again.

Suddenly, you feel your desk raise up into the air. Then something heavy hits the back of your head. You don't know what happens next because you're unconscious. Everything has gone black.

You wake up to a throbbing pain in the back of your head and neck. Your face is covered with dirt, so you wipe it with your sleeve as best you can. You can't see anything at first. Then your eyes adjust.

You're lying on the ground, and something is on top of you. It's something wooden. A door? A desk? You can't tell. You're under a pile of debris. It's too dark to know anything else.

You try to move, but there's a sharp pain in your left leg. The wooden thing has you pinned down.

Suddenly, you hear a voice. It sounds close, but it's muffled. You're not sure who it is.

"Help!" they shout.

You feel trapped, and you want to get this stuff off you. But you're scared that if you move, something might shift and really trap you. It might be best to just stay still and wait.

To wait for help, turn to page 52.
To try to free yourself, turn to page 54.

You decide you'd be better off on your own than trapped inside your tiny school. So you sprint for the door. You hear your teacher shouting your name as you dart off. But soon the sound is drowned out by the roaring storm.

Outside, at the far end of the field, you see the gray clouds approaching. You take off running in the other direction and head toward town. Your family lives at the far end of the small village. You think you can make it there in time.

But as you glance over your shoulder, you see the tornado itself. You squint to see deeper into the clouds. Then you realize there's not just one funnel. There are two!

You can't help but freeze in your tracks. The storm is right on top of the school. You watch as the building shakes. Wood and debris fly everywhere. It looks like the whole building is going to be lifted into the air.

Severe storms can sometimes create multiple funnel clouds that do even more damage.

If you stand here any longer, you'll be next. You turn and run as fast as you can to town. Rain beats down on you. It slaps against your face as you race through it.

You see a church in the distance. Across from it is a large open field. But where should you head?

To hide in the church, turn to page 57.
To run through the field, turn to page 62.

You don't want to risk moving, so you stay put. Your leg hurts, but you can't sit up to see your injuries. You can see a little sunlight creeping through a small crack between two nearby boards. It seems strange for it to be sunny so quickly after the storm passed.

You feel grass under your hands. You're definitely not inside the school. The tornado must have picked you up and dropped you somewhere nearby.

You've heard stories of this sort of thing. Your aunt once told you that her neighbor's cow was plucked up by a tornado. They found it two farms over. It was eating grass as if nothing had happened.

You cough and wipe your mouth. You wonder how long it will take for someone to find you. Your leg feels like it's getting worse.

Hours pass. You keep drifting off to sleep. If someone was coming to help you, surely they would have been here by now. You have no idea that your small town of Biehle has been almost destroyed.

So many are in need of help that your disappearance goes unnoticed. You fall asleep again for the final time. You dream of flying cows and a rescue that never arrives.

THE END

To follow another path, turn to page 9.
To learn more about the Tri-State Tornado, turn to page 101.

You muster all your strength and try to lift the wooden thing on top of you. You raise it just high enough to pull your legs out from underneath. Your left leg doesn't look as bad as you thought. It hurts, but you can move it. It doesn't seem to be broken.

"Help!" you hear someone shout. It's hard to hear them under the debris.

You start pushing boards, bricks, stones, and other objects to dig yourself out. When you push one last broken piece of wood out of your way, the sunlight bursts down on you. You finally climb all the way out of the pile of rubble.

You're in a field. There are broken boards, stones, and bricks everywhere you look. Hundreds of yards behind you is the spot where your school once stood. It's gone. Only the foundation remains.

"Help!" you hear the voice shout again. You look over to find your friend Janet pinned under two broken desks. You push them away and help her to her feet.

"Thanks," she says. Janet doesn't look hurt at all, really. She just has a small scratch on her forehead.

Turn the page.

Several schools, including the one in Biehle, Missouri, and this one in Murphysboro, Illinois, were destroyed.

Eventually, you're reunited with your entire class and your teacher. Amazingly, no one was killed. The entire Garver school and all the students were lifted up and scattered across the nearby fields. Some kids are injured worse than you. Some aren't even bruised. Every one of your friends has survived.

You begin to limp home. You're anxious to see your family. You hope they were as lucky as you and your classmates.

THE END

To follow another path, turn to page 9.
To learn more about the Tri-State Tornado, turn to page 101.

You decide the church might offer some protection. It's better to be inside than to try your luck outside during this storm.

You run to the church and pound on its heavy doors. Then you try the handle. You're in luck—it's not locked.

"Come inside!" says a man from across the room. You recognize him. It's Pastor David. He leads service every Sunday. "Be sure to shut the door behind you!" he shouts.

You rush into the small church. There are several other people there, too. You recognize all of them as neighbors. One is the mother of your friend Sally.

"Get under a pew," says the pastor.

As you crawl under the long wooden bench, you wonder why you ran off from school in the first place. This church is no safer.

Turn the page.

But there's no time to think about that now. You suddenly hear the wind howl unlike anything you've heard before. You look up just in time to see the church's whole roof get ripped right off the walls!

You duck farther under the pew and put your hands over your head. You clench your eyes shut tight. The wind pulls at your clothes and hair.

A loud bang makes your whole body jolt. Looking to your left, you see two pews have crashed into each other. Another is lifting up into the air.

BANG! The pew lands on the other two.

You curl up into the smallest ball you can. You feel yourself sliding, as if the floorboards of the church itself are being lifted. However, you can't bring yourself to look and see what's going on. You're much too frightened.

Even strong brick buildings, such as some schools and churches, were no match for the raging storm.

After less than a minute, it's all over. A strange quiet falls on the room. You sit up. Then you stand. There's almost nothing left of the church.

Turn the page.

There are boards and trash everywhere. Piles of bricks and splintered wood are strewn about the floor and the nearby grounds. You see the pastor help an elderly woman to her feet. A few other people are helping an injured man.

Spread out in front of you are the ruins of your small town, Biehle. It doesn't even look familiar. Trees you've climbed on are now uprooted or split in two. The small swing that hung from a post behind the church is missing.

You have a headache, but otherwise you feel fine. You seem to be one of the lucky ones.

"Fire!" someone yells. "Something's burning!"

You run and climb over one of the church's crumbled walls. You're careful not to hurt yourself. Plenty of broken glass is scattered everywhere.

You run through the churchyard to the nearest road. Where there used to be a row of houses, none remain. A small plume of smoke is rising from the wreckage at the end of the block.

"Fire!" a woman shouts again. You recognize her. It's Mrs. Jeffries. She's standing outside her house, calling for help. In her arms is her two-year-old daughter. But Mrs. Jeffries has twins. You don't see her son anywhere.

"Help!" Mrs. Jeffries yells. "Please, help!"

You look at her, and then glance down the street. At the far end of town, you see another trail of smoke. Could it be coming from your own house? Is your mom there? You wonder if she's okay. Maybe she needs help, too.

To help Mrs. Jeffries, turn to page 64.
To run home instead, turn to page 66.

The church doesn't look any safer than the schoolhouse. So you decide to run through the field back home.

The tall grass crunches under your feet as you sprint. The rain beats down on you harder and harder. Behind you, you hear the tornado. It sounds like a train engine. No, not quite. It sounds like a dozen train engines.

Suddenly, you feel yourself being pulled backward into the air. You feel a sharp pain in your shoulder and hip. Then you're on the ground again. It all happened so fast.

You open your eyes just in time to see a large tree falling directly toward you. It's the last thing you'll ever see.

THE END

To follow another path, turn to page 9.
To learn more about the Tri-State Tornado, turn to page 101.

You're not a firefighter, but you can't just sit by when someone needs help. You run up to Mrs. Jeffries.

"I can't find Jay!" she says in a frantic voice.

There's not much left of her house, but a fire is slowly building in the living room. You try to look inside, but the smoke is thick. You know you can't run in. It would be too dangerous. One of the walls is still standing, and it could collapse at any second.

You race around the outside of the house. The smoke and fire are getting worse. But you can see into the living room clearly now. There's no sign of little Jay.

Then you hear a faint sound behind you. You turn and see a large fallen tree. Its branches are everywhere. They're covered in the first buds of spring.

You hurry over to get a closer look. There's a rustling in the branches. You pull them back as best you can. Underneath them is Jay. He's sitting in the grass and smiling. The little guy seems to actually be enjoying himself.

You pick him up and walk back around the house. Mrs. Jeffries is overjoyed to see her boy. She says something to you, but you can't understand it through her happy sobs. You smile and then race home to check on your own family.

THE END

To follow another path, turn to page 9.
To learn more about the Tri-State Tornado, turn to page 101.

There's nothing you can do for Mrs. Jeffries. You're sure she'll find her son. He probably just wandered off to play with some neighbor kids. You have your own family to think about. So you race down the street toward your house.

Your home was the smallest one downtown. But you're not prepared for what you find. You're overcome with emotion when you see your house is simply gone. All that remains are a few support beams and the broken dresser that used to sit in your parents' bedroom.

Your dad should be at work at the farm outside of town. So you don't expect to find him. But there's no sign of your mother here, either.

You never do learn what happened to her. She might have been trapped somewhere or simply swept away by the storm.

Many homes were destroyed by the storm's powerful winds.

As the months and years pass, your father never gives up hope. Deep down, neither do you. But you never see your mother again. She is one of the many lost in the aftermath of the Tri-State Tornado.

THE END

To follow another path, turn to page 9.
To learn more about the Tri-State Tornado,
turn to page 101.

The tornado destroyed 1,200 buildings and killed 234 people in Murphysboro, Illinois.

CHAPTER 4
THE EDGE OF MURPHYSBORO

The sound of a sputtering engine wakes you from your sleep. You open your eyes and look at the sloped ceiling of your bedroom. Your family lives in a small house outside Murphysboro, Illinois.

Your room takes up the whole top floor. It's basically just a converted attic. But you don't mind. You like the privacy—even though it sometimes gets so hot in the summer that you sneak outside to sleep in the grass.

You glance over at your homemade calendar on the wall. It's March 17, 1925. It probably won't get too hot up there for a few months yet.

Turn the page.

Slowly, your curiosity grows stronger than your need to stay in bed. You get up and walk over to the window. Outside, you see your brother and his best friend, Daniel. They're putting two empty canvas sacks into the back of Daniel's Model T car.

Your brother said Daniel bought the car with his own money. But you've never known him to have a job. He and your brother both dropped out of school in tenth grade. They told your dad they have a mill job outside of town. But they always seem to come home at weird times of the day.

What kind of mill lets you come and go as you please? you wonder

You look at the clock. You're not supposed to wake up for school for another ten minutes. Your brother isn't usually up this early. You put on your school clothes and run outside to see what's happening.

"Hey, Hank!" you call over the sound of the Model T's humming motor.

"Aw, great," says Hank. He smirks and looks at Daniel, who just shrugs. "What are you doing up, squirt?"

"I heard the car," you say. "Going somewhere?"

Turn the page.

Ford Model Ts were one of the most common cars during the 1920s.

"None of your business," says Hank.

"We could use a lookout," says Daniel.

"Hey, knock it off," says Hank. "He doesn't need to be a part of this."

"A part of what?" you ask.

"Ugh, fine," says Hank. "If you're so set on knowing what's what, I'll tell you. But this is just between the three of us, okay? It doesn't get back to Mom and Pop, got it?"

"Okay," you say, without really thinking about it.

"Daniel and I are gonna knock over a bank downtown," says Hank. "It's been real quiet, and we figure we can get in and out without any trouble."

"What? You're kidding, right?" you say, with a big smile on your face.

At first you think Hank is joking. Then your smile fades away. You can tell by Hank's look that he's serious.

"We could use a lookout," says Daniel. "It'd earn you a sawbuck."

A sawbuck? You start thinking about what you could buy with ten whole dollars. It's more than you've ever had. But you're not a criminal. And you can't believe Hank is thinking of doing this either. You could get in trouble or even get thrown in jail. But on the other hand, Hank could be mad if you don't help him out. You're not sure what to do.

To go with Hank and Daniel, turn to page 74.

To tell them you won't help rob the bank, turn to page 77.

You jump in the back of the Model T. Daniel smiles at you, but Hank seems grumpy. You're not sure how your brother got himself into this, but you don't want him to risk his neck alone. If you're the lookout, you might be able to help make sure he doesn't go to jail. Your mom would be heartbroken if her son landed in prison.

Daniel drives you toward Murphysboro. Cities don't get much bigger in this part of Illinois. It's a city of 12,000 people. It's not Chicago, but the city has never failed to impress you. You've lived right outside the city limits all your life. Your dad says that it used to be a simple railroad hub. But the city has taken on a life of its own.

The car slows to a stop as Hank pulls into a parking space. The Ava Bank is down the next block.

"And now, we wait," says Hank.

As you sit in the car, Hank and Daniel keep an eye on the few people coming and going this early in the morning.

Their plan is to wait until the bank president goes out to lunch later in the day. They know that when he's gone, the cashier will be alone in the bank. They plan on storming the place and forcing the cashier to let them into the bank's vault.

Turn the page.

As noon approaches, a man leaves the bank. He walks across the street and shakes hands with a taller man. They head away down the block, apparently toward a local lunch spot.

"That was the bank president," says Daniel. "It's now or never."

He and Hank both put newsboy caps on their heads. They pull the brims down low to hide their faces.

Hank turns to you. "Here we go," he says. But you're still not sure you want to be a part of this plan.

To be Hank and Daniel's lookout, turn to page 78.

To get cold feet and leave, turn to page 81.

"I . . . I can't do it," you finally say.

"C'mon," says Daniel. "You could be our insurance plan. Make sure the cops don't spot us."

"It's fine," says Hank. Daniel looks like he's going to argue further. Then Hank glares at him. Daniel gets quiet.

"Not a word of this to anyone. You hear?" says Hank. He gives you the same look he just gave Daniel.

You watch Hank and Daniel drive off. Then you head back inside.

"Hey, pal," says your dad. He's sitting at the kitchen table with a cup of coffee. "What are you doing up so early?"

To tell your dad what Hank is doing, turn to page 85.

To keep Hank's secret, turn to page 87.

"Okay," says Hank. "Stay in the car. We'll start the engine now, so we can get away quicker. If you see the police, honk the horn three times."

You nod your head. After Daniel starts the car, he and Hank each grab a canvas bag. They walk down the block and then cross the street. You watch as they disappear into the bank.

Bank robberies were very common in Illinois in the mid-1920s.

That's when the guilt starts to creep in. You know what you're doing is wrong. Even if you aren't robbing the bank yourself, it seems just as bad to be the lookout. You don't want to let your brother down. But that money they're stealing doesn't belong to them. And you're helping your brother break the law.

Your palms start to sweat. You keep looking out the back window and from side to side. The street is deserted. That gives you a little relief, at least.

Suddenly, a figure bursts from the bank. Then another follows him. It's Hank and Daniel, and they're in a hurry. Paper bills are fluttering out of the bag Hank is carrying.

You open the doors of the Model T to make it easier for them.

Turn the page.

"Go, go, go!" shouts Hank as Daniel jumps into the driver's seat.

Daniel guns the engine and the car tears down the street. Daniel takes the turns sharp, barely slowing for them at all.

"Not so fast!" shouts Hank. "People will get suspicious!"

Daniel listens and slows down.

"We should head to the hideout and lay low for a few days," says Hank.

"I think we should go home," you say.

"No time for that, kid," says Daniel. "You're in this now, same as us."

To insist on going home,
turn to page 95.

To go to your brother's hideout,
turn to page 97.

Your heart beats faster and faster as you sit in the Model T. You wipe your sweaty palms on your trousers. A car drives by. You nearly jump out of your skin.

That's the last straw, you think. *I'm not cut out for this.*

You leave the car with the engine still running. You just run and keep going until your lungs are burning. Finally, you can't take it anymore. You're not home yet, but that's the last place you want to be. You see an old red barn near the road. You look both ways. The coast is clear. So you head inside.

There has never been a moment in your life where you have felt this unsure. Should you go home? Would your parents know about the robbery somehow? What if Hank has been caught already? What if he tells the police you were involved?

Turn the page.

You don't know what to do, so you look around the empty barn. There's a hayloft above a few dusty tractors. You climb the loft's ladder and sit on a bale of prickly golden straw. You're still breathing heavy from all the running. So you lay down to catch your breath. Before you know it, you've fallen asleep.

You hide in the barn all day. It's all you can think to do. By the following afternoon, you figure it's time to go home. But as you walk outside, a big hailstone hits you on the shoulder. You bend down and pick it up. The cold ball of ice is almost the size of a tennis ball. You've never seen anything like it.

From down the road comes a sound like thunder. You squint and see something that looks like a giant's arm reaching out of the dark clouds and touching the ground.

You quickly realize what you're seeing. It's a tornado! It's coming from the direction of Murphysboro. Your thoughts stray to your brother and Daniel. Where were they? Had they gotten caught in this storm?

You run back into the barn. You crawl under one of the dusty tractors and wait for the storm to pass. Luckily, the tornado doesn't come any closer. It tears down the road in the direction of the neighboring town of DeSoto.

Turn the page.

When you finally make it home, you're relieved to find your house still standing. Hank sends you a postcard from Chicago a few weeks later. He and Daniel made a run for it.

Less than a month later, you learn from your father that both boys were arrested. You make plans to visit Hank in jail, thinking that things could have been much worse. If he had been caught in the tornado, you might never have seen your brother again.

THE END

To follow another path, turn to page 9.
To learn more about the Tri-State Tornado, turn to page 101.

You've never been good at keeping secrets. And you're not about to keep this one if there's a chance your brother could get hurt. So you spill the beans to your dad.

"That kid," your father grumbles under his breath. "Do you know which bank?"

"Oh, uh . . . no. They didn't say," you tell him.

"Is it in Murphysboro?"

"I don't know," you say. "Maybe."

"Well, do you have any idea of where they'll go to next?" asks your dad.

You think about it, but you can only shake your head. Hank has told you many times of a place he called his "secret hideout." It was supposed to be near the unfinished railroad tracks, not far from the outskirts of Murphysboro. You're pretty sure you could find it if you had enough time.

Turn the page.

"I'm going to go look for him," says your dad. "You head to school, you hear?"

You do as you're told, but when you get home after school, there's still no sign of Hank. By the next morning, he still hasn't come home. You feel like you have to do something. You'd bet anything that he's lying low at his hideout. You could go there, but you'd have to skip out on school. You're not sure what to do.

To go to Hank's secret hideout, turn to page 89.

To go to school instead, turn to page 93.

"Oh, just . . . " you say, hesitating, ". . . nothing."

Your dad gives you a strange look. "Was that Hank outside?" he asks.

"Yeah," you say. "I think he's going to work."

"He's a hardworking kid when he wants to be," says your father.

"Um, Dad?" you say. Your voice is shaky as you speak. "Can I stay home from school today? I don't feel too good." It's not a lie. You feel sick with guilt.

The next day, you feel the same. Hank hasn't returned home, and you're not sure he will anytime soon. You stay in bed and continue to pretend to be sick. Eventually, you fall asleep.

You wake up to muffled shouting. You rush downstairs.

Turn the page.

"There's been a tornado!" says your father. "Downtown is a disaster area. Do you know where your brother is?"

You decide to finally tell your dad everything. But it's too late. You never hear from your brother again. Three weeks later, your brother's body is found in a destroyed shack by the abandoned railroad tracks. He and Daniel were both killed by the storm. And the money they stole is never found.

THE END

To follow another path, turn to page 9.
To learn more about the Tri-State Tornado, turn to page 101.

It's after 2:00 p.m. when you cross over a culvert near Hank's hideout. It's just a small wooden shed that leans a little to one side. That must be why it was abandoned by whomever built it.

As you head toward the shed, you notice the air feels cooler than before. Suddenly, you feel a sting at the base of your neck. You reach into your collar and pull out something cold and hard. When you look closer, you realize it's a big hailstone.

Before you can think about its unusual size, you hear a familiar motor. A Model T is fast approaching down the dirt road.

The car pulls to a quick stop in front of you. Through a dust cloud, you can see your brother.

"Get inside!" he shouts, jumping out of the car. He seems scared. Maybe the police have found him. He and Daniel run by you and into the wooden shack. They don't seem to care you're here.

Turn the page.

"Come on!" Hank shouts from the shed's open door. "Get in here!"

As you hurry toward him, you're pelted by more hailstones.

"Shut the door!" Daniel shouts from across the small room.

You move to the door. But just as you're about to shut it, you see what has your brother so spooked. It's not the police that he's worried about.

Down the road and across a field, you see a large dark cloud. It's like nothing you've ever seen before. You strain your eyes and look closer. You see a funnel swirling at the fog's center. It's a huge tornado!

You glance back at your brother and Daniel. They're huddling under the tiny table in the center of the room. There's no way this shack will protect you from the storm.

Before you realize what you're doing, you sprint toward the culvert. You run beneath the small stone bridge and huddle on top of a pile of rocks. The wind whips around you. But you don't move. You try to make your body as small as you can.

A short time later, the roaring wind dies down. You gather all of your courage. Then you stand up, dust yourself off, and climb out of the culvert.

Turn the page.

The sun is already shining again. But that's not what you notice first. You're too busy looking at the spot where Hank's hideout used to be. All that remains is a pile of broken boards.

Both your brother and Daniel were killed in the tornado. As you walk back home, a light breeze picks up. In front of you, a few loose dollar bills blow by. They're all that's left of the robbery. You walk by them and let the wind carry them where it will.

THE END

To follow another path, turn to page 9.
To learn more about the Tri-State Tornado, turn to page 101.

The last thing you want to do is make your dad angry by not obeying his orders. So you pack your schoolbag and go about your day as usual.

Unfortunately, the day has different plans.

You spend most of it worrying about your brother. But around 2:45 p.m., you stop thinking about him when you see something fly by the school's window. You take another look and see a hailstone hit the windowsill. Then another. And another.

You're about to tell the teacher, but then you see something off in the distance. A dark cloud is moving steadily toward the school. And inside spins the funnel of a giant tornado.

"Tornado!" someone yells before you can.

The kids around you begin to panic. You're not sure if you should hide under your desk or run. But you never get the chance to do either.

Turn the page.

Seconds later, the roof of the school collapses in on you and your classmates. In your last moments, your thoughts stray again to your brother. You can only hope that he's safe wherever he is.

THE END

To follow another path, turn to page 9.
To learn more about the Tri-State Tornado, turn to page 101.

It takes a few minutes of nagging, but Daniel finally gives in. He barely slows to a stop when you reach your house. You jump out of the Model T, kicking up dust when your feet hit the dirt lane.

"Not a word of this to anyone," warns Hank.

You head inside and go up to your room. Filled with guilt, you stay there all day. When your parents get back, you tell them you stayed home because you felt sick.

The next morning, your parents ask if you know where Hank is. You tell them you don't.

Later that day, that statement becomes all too true when a huge tornado unexpectedly rips through town. It destroys nearly all of Murphysboro.

Turn the page.

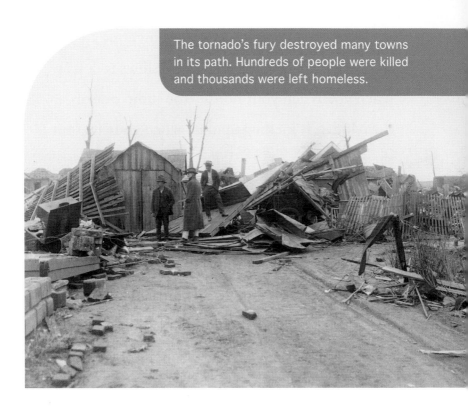

The tornado's fury destroyed many towns in its path. Hundreds of people were killed and thousands were left homeless.

You never find out if Hank was caught in the tornado, or if he simply left town. Either way, it doesn't change the guilt you feel for the rest of your life.

THE END

To follow another path, turn to page 9.
To learn more about the Tri-State Tornado,
turn to page 101.

You decide you don't feel like going home and being alone. So you stay in the car and head to your brother's hideout. Soon enough, the Model T pulls up to a nearly collapsed wooden shack next to some abandoned railroad tracks.

"Let's count the loot!" says Daniel in an excited voice. Hank laughs, and the two head inside. You follow them into the small shack. There are a few blankets on the floor and a couple pots and pans in the corner.

"Don't worry," says Hank. "We'll only be here a couple of days."

Only a couple of days? you think nervously.

* * *

The next day you feel your stomach growling fiercely. You haven't eaten since before yesterday.

"Are we ever going to get something to eat?" you ask.

Turn the page.

"You're welcome to try any time you want," says Hank. He points to the fishing poles leaning against the corner of the shed.

You grab one and head outside. Right away, you feel the wind pulling at the fishing pole in your hand. You stare in shock down the dirt road. A tornado is spinning in the distance—and it's heading right for you!

You run back into the shack, but it's too late. The last thing you see is a cloud of dust and dirt, as you feel yourself being hurled through the air.

THE END

To follow another path, turn to page 9.
To learn more about the Tri-State Tornado, turn to page 101.

Griffin, Indiana, was destroyed by the terrible storm.

CHAPTER 5
THE TORNADO'S AFTERMATH

After three and a half hours, the Tri-State Tornado had traveled more than 200 miles (320 km) between Ellington, Missouri and Princeton, Indiana. It's believed the tornado sped along at 62 to 73 miles (100 to 117 km) per hour across the land. The Tri-State Tornado lasted so long, many experts still wonder if it was really multiple twisters instead.

The devastation left by the tornado can't be overstated. Survivors said there was simply nothing left. Even the foundations of some buildings were carried away. Fires broke out, making a terrible situation even worse. In Murphysboro, Illinois, the storm cut off the town's water supply, leaving firefighters helpless.

As in most tragedies, help eventually arrived. With no modern ambulances or helicopters, most rescuers and supplies arrived by train. The American Red Cross gave tents to those without homes for temporary shelter. Food and other basic necessities were handed out.

After the storm passed, emergency relief camps gave out food and aid to survivors.

People from all over the country gave money to help restore the damaged areas. Yet most of these towns never fully recovered. When they did rebuild, many residents constructed storm cellars first.

U.S. Air Force weathermen Major Ernest Fawbush and Captain Robert Miller led the charge for tornado detection. In 1948 a tornado touched down at Tinker Air Force Base near Oklahoma City, Oklahoma. Miller and Fawbush investigated the weather conditions and came up with a way to predict tornadoes that still works to this day.

Miller and Fawbush's method was soon used nationwide. Thanks to the work of these two men, countless lives have been saved. Cities now know in advance when a tornado is on its way.

A huge and powerful tornado hit Joplin, Missouri, on May 22, 2011. The deadly twister killed 158 people and caused at least $2.8 billion of damage.

Today, warnings tell people to seek out shelter or evacuate an area. These warnings have helped prevent tornado-related injuries and deaths from reaching the same tragic numbers as the 1925 Tri-State Tornado.

In the modern world, communication and transportation are both easier than ever. Thanks to science and modern warning systems, it's unlikely that a tornado will ever claim as many lives as the Tri-State Tornado.

Tornadoes are still a natural phenomenon to be feared and respected. But humans have adapted to meet the challenges they present. If we continue to respect nature and pursue scientific knowledge, the deadliest tornado in human history will remain a thing of the past.

MORE ABOUT THE
PATH OF THE STORM

The Tri-State Tornado traveled across three states: Missouri, Illinois, and Indiana. Every town in its path was caught unprepared, yet death tolls ranged wildly as the storm seemed to gather or lose strength. The tornado was thought to be at least 1 mile (1.6 km) wide in some parts of its journey. More than 15,000 homes were destroyed and 695 people were killed by the Tri-State Tornado before it disappeared.

ILLINOIS

MISSOURI

MURPHYSBORO
40% destroyed
234 deaths

DE SOTO
30% destroyed
69 deaths

BIEHLE
100% destroyed
4 deaths

ANNAPOLIS
90% destroyed
4 deaths

INDIANA

PRINCETON
25% destroyed
45 deaths

GRIFFIN
100% destroyed
25 deaths

KENTUCKY

OTHER PATHS TO EXPLORE

>>> It took a while for the Red Cross and other rescue workers to arrive in the towns destroyed by the Tri-State Tornado. If you were a survivor who made it through unharmed, what would you do to help those in need? Would you offer your homeless neighbors a place to stay or volunteer to help watch younger children? What could you do to help those affected by the storm?

>>> The Tri-State Tornado tore through the Mississippi River. Some people reported seeing fish fall from the air after being sucked into the storm's funnel. Imagine you're in a boat on the river as the storm strikes. What other things might you have witnessed? Do you think you would have seen the signs of a tornado early enough to dock your boat? Or would you have been caught by surprise like the people of neighboring villages?

>>> Travel wasn't as easy in 1925 as it is today. Even so, many people still ventured far from home to visit family or friends from time to time. Imagine you were visiting family in Indiana when the tornado hit on March 18, and you didn't know what to do. What would be your first reaction? Where would you go during a storm if you weren't familiar with the neighborhood? Would you trust strangers to help you?

BIBLIOGRAPHY

Castleden, Rodney. *Natural Disasters That Changed the World*. Edison, NJ: Chartwell Books, 2007.

The History Channel: *The Wrath of God: Disasters in America: Tornado Alley*. https://www.youtube.com/watch?v=hJ6Z1CV704I

Lusted, Marcia Amidon. *The 12 Worst Tornadoes of All Time*. Mankato, MN: 12-Story Library, 2019.

Spilsbury, Louise and Richard. *Terrifying Tornadoes*. Chicago: Heinemann Library, 2010.

Tarshis, Lauren. *Tornado Terror*. New York: Scholastic Inc., 2017.

Williams, Dinah. *Terrible But True: Awful Events in American History*. New York: Scholastic Inc., 2016.

GLOSSARY

bismuth (BIZ-muhth)—a metallic compound used in some medicines to calm stomach issues

cellar (SEH-luhr)—a basement or underground room usually used for storing food or other items

culvert (KUHL-vuhrt)—a tunnel under a road or railroad that allows water to drain

debris (duh-BREE)—the scattered pieces of something that has been broken or destroyed

foundation (fown-DAY-shuhn)—a solid structure on which a building is built

phenomenon (fih-NAH-muh-nahn)—something very unusual or remarkable

plume (PLOOM)—a long cloud of smoke or vapor resembling a feather

primitive (PRIH-muh-tiv)—simple or not advanced

queasiness (KWEE-zee-nuhss)—the feeling of having an upset or sick stomach

sawbuck (SAW-buhk)—an old word for a 10-dollar bill

stifle (STYE-fuhl)—to cover up or stop oneself from making a sound

unprecedented (uhn-PREH-suh-den-tuhd)—never experienced or known before

READ MORE

Crane, Cody. *All About Tornadoes*. New York: Children's Press, 2021.

Hubbard, Ben. *Hurricanes and Tornadoes*. London: Franklin Watts, 2019.

Lusted, Marcia Amidon. *The 12 Worst Tornadoes of all Time*. Mankato, MN: 12-Story Library, 2019.

Tarshis, Lauren. *Tornado Terror*. New York: Scholastic Inc., 2017.

INTERNET SITES

Britannica: The Tri-State Tornado of 1925
britannica.com/event/Tri-State-Tornado-of-1925

History.com: The Tri-State Tornado
history.com/this-day-in-history/the-tri-state-tornado

National Geographic Kids: Tornado Facts!
natgeokids.com/uk/discover/geography/physical-geography/tornado-facts/

ABOUT THE AUTHOR

Author photo courtesy of Dorothy Manning Photography.

Matthew K. Manning is the author of more than 90 books and dozens of comic books. Some of his favorite projects include the popular comic book crossover *Batman/ Teenage Mutant Ninja Turtles Adventures* and the 12-issue series *Marvel Action: Avengers* for IDW, *Exploring Gotham City* for Insight Editions, and the six-volume chapter book series *Xander and the Rainbow-Barfing Unicorns* for Capstone. Manning lives in Asheville, North Carolina with his wife Dorothy and their two kids, Lillian and Gwendolyn. Visit him online at www.matthewkmanning.com.